The Book of Ocean

This is a work of poetry. Any resemblance to real persons, living or dead, or actual events is purely coincidental — unless it was meant to be remembered.

For more information, please contact:

author@k-mondal.com

"And the ocean kept everything we could never say."

Completed on: 22 July 2025

By

K.M. Drayven

The Book of Ocean

K.M. Drayven

I know you've forgotten me.

But who am I, really?

The one who waited for you in silence

The one who always tried to stay beside you

The one who simply tried to love you

Yes, I know you've forgotten me

But when I look up at the stars

I still remember you

Because in this busy life

those are the moments

when I see the sky

when I see the stars

that I long to see you

But in my imagination

I could never complete you

So I, I chose the sky

In a corner of the emptiness

I try to clear my own thoughts

The things I once promised myself

to imagine

Everywhere I go

I feel the presence of darkness

I speak to myself softly

asking

Is the light of darkness still here

In this selfish reality

I reach for a memory

where I was the enemy

of my own story

In a world where people use you

In a world where you fight against yourself

In a silence where no vibration can reach you

The “you”

is the source of your own power

The power that once bloomed

into something beautiful—

a flower

The rose of war

Where you are the victim

and the situation becomes your only sympathy

Where pain must be felt

but never resisted

And I see you

more beautiful than you know

If the war comes

take the flower—

because even the grave

deserves to look beautiful

The soul

The one I carry

but never stop to see

The soul with a heart

that no one ever feels

Because it hides too deep

behind silence and memory

The memory every time came to hit

The memory that was able to kill

I was that soul

breaking pieces of myself

just to feel something

just to ask

Why me

The drop of water whispered

And the wind answered back

Because you are the one

who turned a tear into a diamond

And the one

who made a life

into a song

You are always with me, beside me, within me,

I can't see you,

But I feel you,

You are the darkness, and I am the light.

Still you stay with me, always at my side.

When the wind heard her voice,

it spoke to the cloud with aching grace:

"I will show you the beauty of a bond,

a connection deeper than sound or sight."

But the bond ended when the one who held it

was no longer there to carry its light.

And in that darkness, something remained

—

a silence that shimmered, a grief that shined.

Because from that sorrow a glow was born,

brighter than the sun ever dared to rise.

I In the war of law, I had no power, but still I stood.

My blood spilled, and I wasn't even allowed to think about it.

I stayed— not because I had to, but because I chose to.

The one standing before me was the one who once fed me rice,

the same one who stood beside me when I had nothing at all.

When you die, you rise— so don't speak if you fight.

Just stand with me, and I'll be at your side.

Who will tell the world how a soldier was killed without a name?

I woke from the dream and touched my father's hand.

Then I walked alone into the war,

because now...

it's time to rise.

You know your eyes.

I've seen them many times.

You're beautiful in a way that only eternity could explain.

Don't look at me—because you are divine,

even from far away.

It's hard not being close.

You're like a violin, I'm like a star,

and your voice is the sound of water I long to hear.

Everyone wants to hear it—

but when I do, it breaks my thoughts into pieces.

Because you are far from me,

happy in your life,

and I am just happy thinking of you.

The word of you is enough to keep me alive.

Not the life I lived before death,

but the one I carry in my grave.

Thank you for the memory that now bleeds.

And the sunflower that chose to stay.

The crown city — where people smile like prayers,

where joy is the key that unlocks every blessing.

It's the city I was meant to find,

where breath moves with the wind,

and letters sleep in the dirt while faces stay locked in rooms.

If imagination stops, the city goes silent.

Only sketches remain, and echoes fade into cold waves.

We smile — but not in life —

we smile in light, the light that came

after the nuclear fire kissed the earth.

Still, the city lives.

It holds our names in its cracked walls,

because we were born to make it ours.

The Days Pass.

The line that's never been touched,

the one that binds everything.

The line you never dared to cross,

the one that speaks the truth—

if only a single step could cross it.

The line that waited

for someone to arrive and cross.

The line never forgotten

because of us.

The line that should've stayed invisible…

but maybe it never was.

Maybe we created it.

Was it really the line's fault

or the person who crossed?

Or maybe

that line was the beginning

of where every step

started to count.

See the soul

The soul with infinite life

The one that longs to speak with you

It is the soul that lived

before the beginning of time

These are the souls

that only speak truth

They are still alive

formless

pure energy

and they are yours

If your soul becomes the path

and your body walks it

then you are the traveller

and your soul is the light

I am not a human, but I wonder if you know how it feels to be bound by a chain — not made of metal, but of silence, of memory, of something that lives in your blood. A chain that never breaks, a chain you cannot see, yet it holds you close, tightening when you try to grow, when you try to speak — and all that escapes is pain, unspoken, unshared, a quiet ache that becomes your shadow.

Still, I stay. Still, I grow. If I never see the world, I send my seeds in my place — each one carrying a hope, a piece of me, a new beginning. But even then, wherever they fall, wherever I take root, the chain returns — soft, invisible, eternal — wrapped around my being like old sunlight.

It is the chain every tree is born with, the one that travels through soil and soul, the one that never ends, and always begins again.

A stone, just a stone — a thing without breath, without story, without name. It lay silent beneath the sky, seen by all, felt by none. Thrown into water, it made no cry, but it hurt — the impact changed its shape, softened its edges, carved it with time and the memory of touch.

Still lifeless, still silent, yet something began to grow. From the stillness, from the wounds, it found a calm that the world never gave it. And one day, a flower bloomed in its hand — yes, the stone held a flower, and looked to the sky, not as a thing, but as something alive.

Everyone had touched it, stepped over it, forgotten it — but it had never broken. Only changed. Only waited. The stone, once nothing, had become life. A soul. A heart. A quiet blessing in the shape of stillness.

A crack that never fully heals —

that's the crack where everything begins.

The crack that forces you to live,

from the edge of breaking to the beginning of light.

The crack that teaches you pain and grace,

helps you gain a new moment, a new sense.

It's a long journey to fill it,

but even when it's filled,

it remains —

not as a wound,

but as a memory.

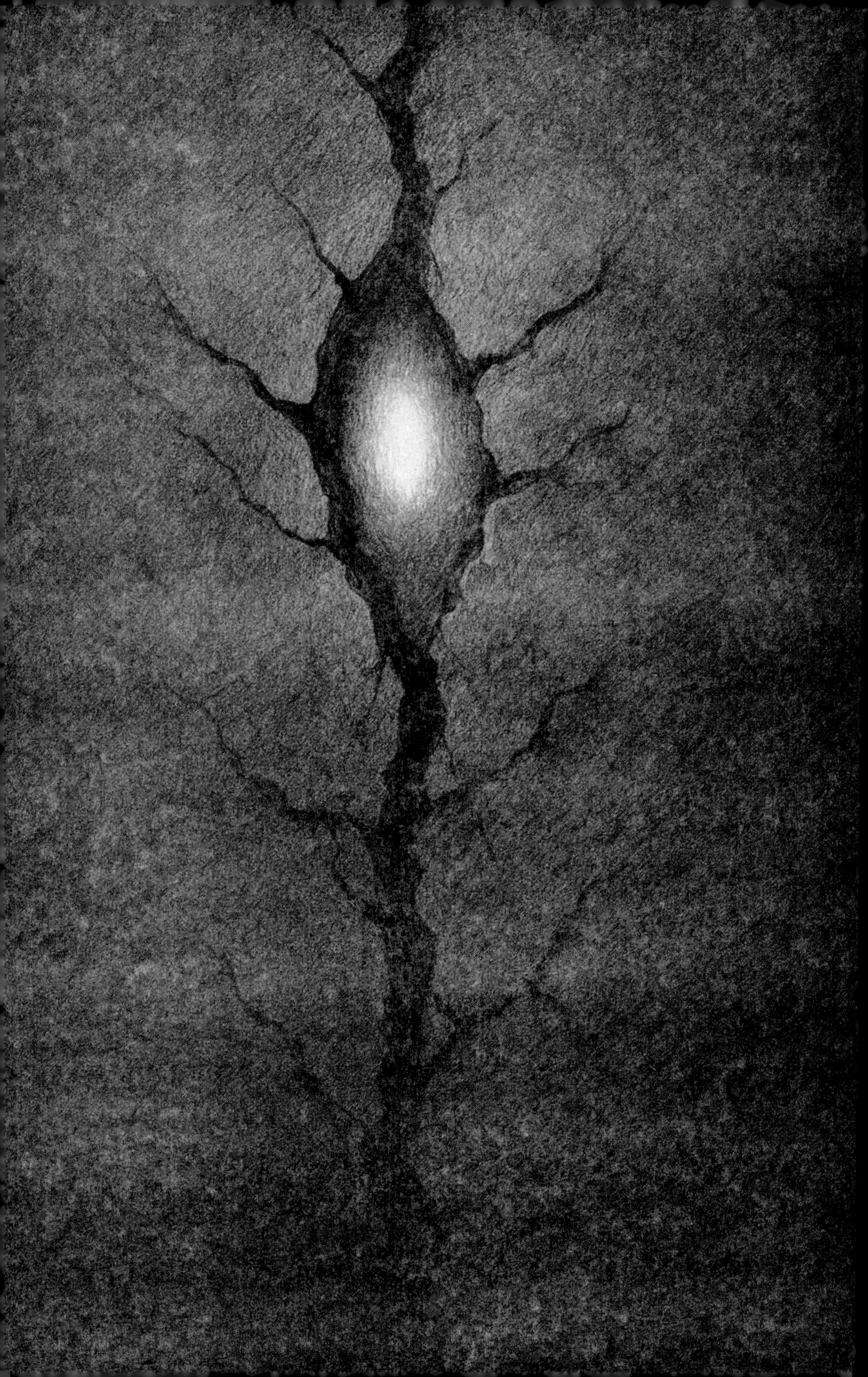

An Eye That Guides Me

An eye that guides me,

an eye that sees me —

makes me safe, makes me clean.

An eye that never turns away,

never ignores,

holding my every step like a quiet prayer.

In its gaze,

I find the courage to grow,

to shape myself in silence.

An eye that never blinks when I break,

that never shivers when I fall.

Yet it shines —

more beautiful,

more tender,

than even you.

The Path That Chose Me

The path I walk was already chosen

The hope I burn within my chest

it too was chosen

I stood at the highest peak

and still, I asked

Where am I truly chosen?

It's a path that scorches the soul

but I shone in my hope

unshaken even in the flames

Then one day, you came to me

And I knew

the guidance I gave wasn't destiny

it was worth

The hope I saw in you was worth

The bond we built

not fate but worth

Let's sit together.

Feel the sensation of the word,

the way it arrives — let's hold it.

Through a thousand lifetimes, you never spoke,

but you gave everything.

And in that quiet,

your silence roared louder than all.

You were never chosen for strength —

you were chosen for hope.

And when all meaning fades,

I look up,

and see a star.

Not a desire,

but a hope —

guiding,

pure,

eternal.

Music Was a Flow

Music was a flow.

When the flow touched rhythm,

a feeling appeared — quiet, powerful, alive.

The music you created was supreme.

When its frequency reached the heart,

it changed everything.

It softened storms.

It bloomed silence.

Like a flower that suddenly appears —

from nowhere,

from everything.

When the truth says, "I am lonely,"

the lie trembles.

When the truth whispers, "I am in trouble,"

the lie laughs.

There comes a day

when the truth begins to wear a mask,

and the lie walks free —

dressed in honesty.

Words lose their weight

when truth gives her soul to the lie.

And in that moment,

a quiet crack begins to spread.

They remain —

the truth,

and her lie.

Bound not by honesty or deception,

bound by the pain of becoming one.

truth
lie

A sword once killed a man.

The same sword made another rise. But the blade we carry now — it's not held in our hands. It's hidden in our hearts, wrapped in silence, shaped by choice.

A sword is not freedom.

It's a burden dressed in shine; a decision folded into steel.

Each day we wield its word,

not to cut skin but to slice the soul.

A whisper becomes the blade. A sentence, the wound.

And not every knife draws blood — some break the heart in pieces too small to name.

We speak, and the word becomes the sword.

It shields us when we're weak, hides us when we're afraid,

builds walls we never meant to raise.

But when the word fails — when it cannot protect, or defend, or free all that remains is the silence,

that the sword was never ours.

It was chosen.

And we, simply, were the ones who bled.

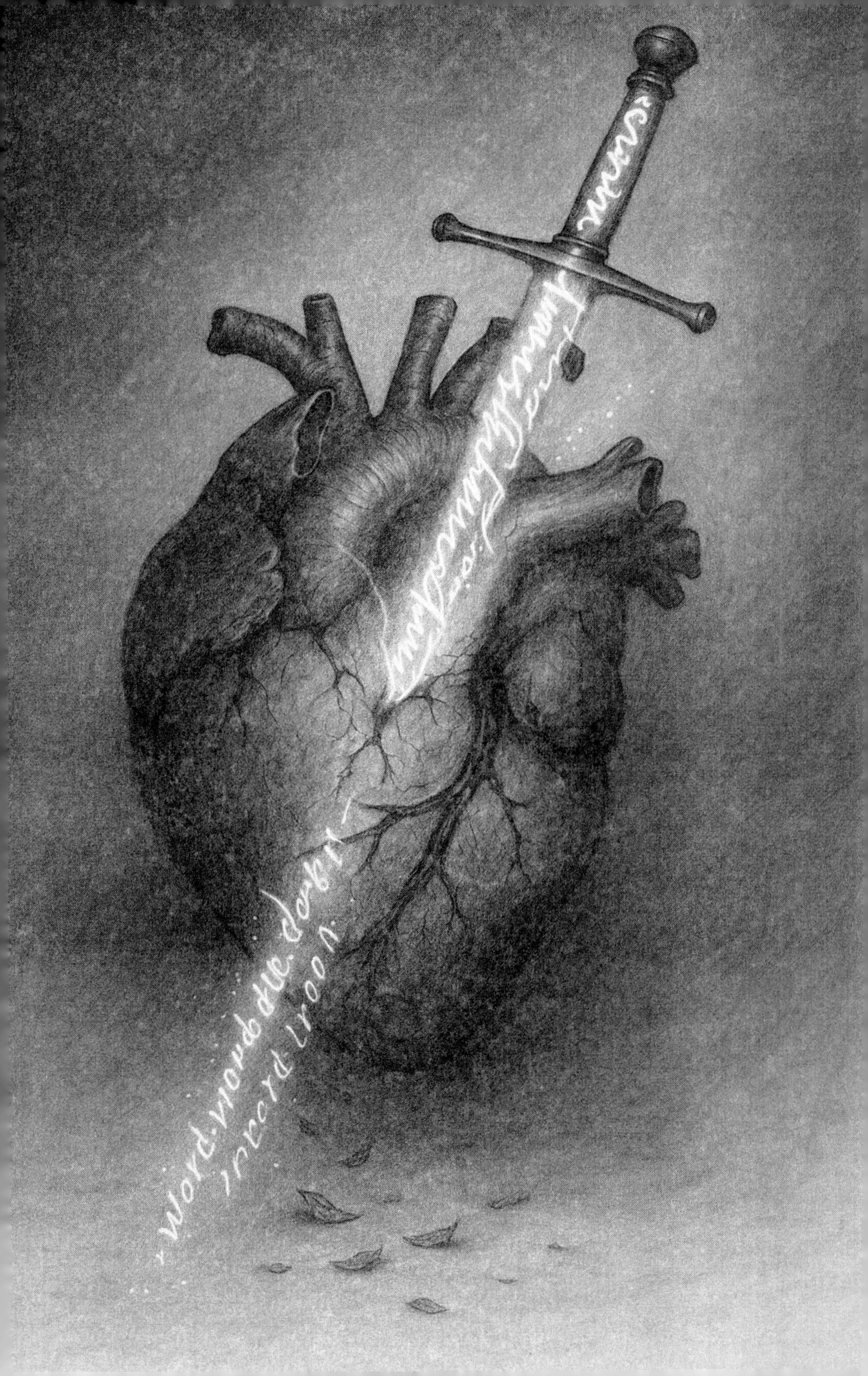

The feeling turns into sensation
when the key of the atmosphere speaks.
When the air hums with connection,
and the heart remembers
someone it never forgot.
The feeling becomes warmth,
and warmth becomes light —
when a joyful face
meets the silence of the universe.
When you see me
I feel you in memory, something stirs.
In the mind,
your thought arrives like a wave
and collapses everything
into one single pulse.
That pulse
is the sensation I feel.
And I imagine.

History of the Forbidden

Someone died —

not to win,

but simply to lose.

In that loss,

a bond was born,

etched into the cracks of time.

The moment shattered

in a single breath.

The forbidden blurred into illusion,

and the truth —

it faded,

became

history.

The Symbol Without Voice

Never heard the voice you use,

yet the symbol still touched me.

When thoughts begin to vanish,

it is then —

the symbol reveals itself.

A moment

where everything begins again.

A world watches

as a new soul is born.

When vision sees not habit,

but presence,

judgment fades.

Still,

it is the symbol.

And it speaks,

without a voice.

The Season We Forgot

The atmosphere shifted

with a lotus in bloom —

heavy,

as if carrying all the things

we could never say.

In the ache of not seeing each other,

something whispered,

"We returned."

The days passed slowly,

but the season stayed beautiful,

even when

it was gone.

Even when

we forgot to remember.

The Role We Both Play

When a role hides pain,

it's not just you concealing —

it's me, watching.

When your effort gives everything,

and your gentle hands still feed me,

the love you offer

is more than words can carry.

It's not everything I want to know —

just the part you try to hide.

Because pain like yours

can't be fully spoken.

Being a parent is hard —

almost impossible to describe.

But in this role,

we live the same life.

And in that life,

nothing truly hides.

A thought was like a glowworm —

not made for darkness,

but alive within it.

And when the moment felt right,

it glowed.

The glowworm sat in a room,

quietly beautiful —

isn't it?

They never thought of why,

they just gave light

in every direction.

Beautiful,

simply for being.

Like that —

an action taken,

a quiet choice —

can turn a glowworm

into a sun-plant.

The joy that can't be fulfilled

The joy that once always returned

The joy that is priceless

yet somehow carries a price

It is the telegraph where everything changed

It is the moment when time held its breath

The feeling that gives life

even when life forgets how to feel

It takes everything

or it gives everything

The joy

still breathing

in silence

waiting to be seen

by the one who never arrived

but was always meant to

The ending comes near

when something begins to breathe

It's only sympathy

that learns how to hold on too long

When the moon whispers to her scars

they write their own story

in the language of silence

and they stay

together

Not perfect—

but accepting

like the wind

seen only in how it moves the world

The feelings were too deep

like an ocean

Too vast to imagine

too sacred to speak

too delicate to store in memory

It was the sound of wings that never fall

a silence louder than the storms we carry

It gave the truth

a truth never written

never spoken

only felt

It was deep

deep like an ocean

and still

it lives in us

Hope never dies — it's written.

9 789334 362152

Printed at Repro India Ltd.